# THE
## *Archive Photographs*
### SERIES

# HAMPSTEAD
# GARDEN SUBURB
## PAST AND PRESENT

'Rus in Urbe', the integration of country and town was an abiding theme of the design of Garden Cities and Garden Suburbs. Within a few years of its construction in 1909, Asmuns Hill had created the image of 'Utopia NW11'.

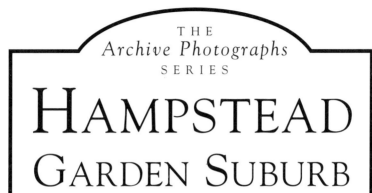

THE
*Archive Photographs*
SERIES

# HAMPSTEAD
## GARDEN SUBURB
### PAST AND PRESENT

*Compiled by*
Mervyn Miller

⁝HAMPSTEAD · GARDEN · SVBVRB · TRUST⁝

CHALFORD

First published 1995
Copyright © Dr Mervyn Miller, 1995

The Chalford Publishing Company
St Mary's Mill, Chalford,
Stroud, Gloucestershire, GL6 8NX

ISBN 0 7524 0319 2

Typesetting and origination by
The Chalford Publishing Company
Printed in Great Britain by
Redwood Books, Trowbridge

*To Stuart Gray for revealing the 'Pisgah sight'*

Willifield Way looking south to the Club Housec, c.1912.

# Contents

# Acknowledgements

I should like to thank Christopher Kellerman, Manager of Hampstead Garden Suburb Trust; Harry Cobb, Hampstead Garden Suburb Archivist; Richard Wakefield of HGS Residents Association; Rev. Alan Walker and the PCC of the Parish Church of St Jude-on-the-Hill; Rev. A.J. Spring of The Free Church; Memories, Hendon; Jane Whitton, Terry Rand, David Bogush and all who assisted in making material available and supporting the preparation of this book. Sheila Murray's patient transcription of the text and captions eased the stress of finalising the manuscript.

# Introduction

'The most nearly perfect example of that English invention and speciality, the Garden Suburb'. So wrote the eminent architectural historian Sir Nikolaus Pevsner in the Hampstead Garden Suburb Golden Jubilee Programme in 1957. The founder, Dame Henrietta Barnett (1851-1936) would have welcomed this plaudit, but with the rejoinder that she had laboured to bring the 'homes of democracy within a tuppenny tube journey from inner London', and to create a community where barriers of social class could be broken down.

The Suburb had been created through enlightened self-interest. Canon Barnett, her husband, had been Vicar of St Jude's Whitechapel, in the heart of the most notorious East End London slums from the 1870s. The Barnetts had acquired Heath End House, near Whitestone Pond, above Hampstead Heath, and this provided respite for themselves and many of their flock. In 1896 they learned of the proposal to construct the Charing Cross, Euston and Hampstead Railway, the first of the deep underground lines, and in 1902, Parliamentary sanction was granted for its construction with an extension to Golders Green, by a syndicate led by the American, Charles Tyson Yerkes. The Barnetts foresaw the unspoilt fields north of Wyldes Farm being covered with bricks and mortar. Drawing on the Commons Registration Movement, led by Octavia Hill, with whom Henrietta Barnett had worked in the East End, it was decided to preserve a Hampstead Heath extension of eighty acres, and ultimately to develop 'a garden suburb for all classes' on the surrounding land.

Mrs Barnett approached the owners, Eton College, to negotiate an option to purchase, only to be told 'you are only a woman ... now if you could get a few men behind you ... everything would be all right'. Nonplussed, she organised her syndicate of eight, two earls, two lawyers, two free churchmen, a bishop and a woman (herself). The others were the Earl of Crewe, Earl Grey, Sir John Gorst, Sir Robert Hunter, Herbert Marnham, Walter Hazell, and the Bishop of London, Dr Winnington Ingram. The purchase was confirmed, and on 2 May 1907, a large gathering in a field east of Finchley Road witnessed Henrietta Barnett turn the sod for the development of the seventy acre 'Artisans' Quarter'. The spade was handed to her by Raymond Unwin (1863-1940), who had prepared the layout plan, and designed many of the early cottages for the Co-Partnership Tenants, a pioneer organisation in building working-class housing. The overall plan and design of the Suburb was shaped by the experience of the First Garden City at Letchworth, Hertfordshire, developed from 1904 to a layout by Barry Parker and Raymond Unwin.

Henrietta Barnett herself had selected the site for the centre with its churches and institute, and glimpses towards the Heath Extension. Unwin's earliest, 1905 plan, indicated a villagey group including shops and a club house. In 1908 a more formal concept emerged, designed by Edwin Lutyens (1869-1944). Construction of the familiar trinity of St Jude's, the Free Church and The Institute began 1909-11, supremely confident Lutyens's designs, with a touch of pomp and circumstance, which did not entirely please Mrs Barnett, who engineered Lutyens dismissal by the Co- Partners, for the extravagance of the North Square houses. Lutyens's influence was widely seen in the work of G.L. Sutcliffe, J.C.S. Soutar, Michael Bunney, Herbert Welch and Cowles Voysey, and even Parker and Unwin, contrasting with the Arts and Crafts informality of their earlier work, and that by M.H. Baillie Scott, who designed Waterlow Court flats for single ladies, Courtenay Crickmer and Geoffry Lucas.

The work of a Who's Who of domestic architecture formed a backcloth for life in the Suburb. Through the lenses of early photographers we can now appreciate the freshness of the buildings in their settings before the car reigned supreme. We can revisit the Club House, fatally damaged in 1940, or St Jude's before Walter Starmer's murals appeared; see the pageants and masques, witness life in Waterlow Court or The Orchard and follow Royalty on their many visits, often accompanied by the indefatigable Dame Henrietta Barnett. Children at school and at play evoke a less stressful era. The development of the 'New Suburb', spreading north and east began hesitantly just before the First World War and burgeoned afterwards as did car ownership, and traffic on the expediently upgraded Falloden Way-Lyttelton Road, constructed as a link to the Barnet By-pass in the 1920s. Henrietta Barnett died in 1936, and did not see the damage caused by wartime bombs and land mines.

Post War recovery took the Suburb to its Golden Jubilee, which established a pattern for commemoration. The 'old Trust', founded by Mrs Barnett, was out-manoeuvred in the cut and thrust of 1960s property dealing, and the Suburb as a whole was offered for sale in 1969. Through the initiative of the HGS Protection Society and the Residents' Association, the Trust was reconstituted in 1972, and still fulfils its landlord obligation to preserve the environment of the Suburb. The London Borough of Barnet, in whose area the Suburb had been since 1965, designated it as a Conservation Area in 1968, and obtained strict planning powers 'to preserve or enhance its architectural and historic interest'. Most residents are conscious of their personal responsibility to uphold standards, and the visual quality of the Suburb is now world-renowned.

The 'spirit of the place' lives on in events such as 'Suburb Weekend', which brings the community together in a manner which would have gladdened Mrs Barnett's heart. Regrettably, few 'artisans' remain in the desirable cottage quarter, and larger houses in Winnington Road change hands for millions, often to absentee owners. The buoyancy of the property market over the past ninety years has ensured the economic viability of the development, but Henrietta's dream, Utopia NW11, has become, perhaps inevitably, largely a preserve of the wealthy middle-class. This record in photographs spanning almost 90 years will, it is hoped, help to rekindle some aspects of the idealism upon which the whole development was founded.

Dr Mervyn Miller, September 1995

# One
# Henrietta Barnett's Vision

The squalor of Whitechapel in the East End of London with its airless insanitary slum courts and rife disease and crime, was the target of housing reformers and public health legislators in the late 19th century.

North London stopped abruptly short of the ridge which terminated Hampstead Heath. Beyond lay virgin countryside including wooded heathland and centuries' old farmsteads. On the slopes north of St Jude's Cottage, Hampstead Heath, and Erskine House convalescent home, for the sick and weary from the East End, stand Canon and Mrs Henrietta Barnett, her invalid sister Miss Fanny Rowland and Miss Gale, dwarfed by the majestic Turner's pines. Fear of indiscriminate development of this land prompted Henrietta Barnett's action.

Henrietta Barnett (1851-1936) had, as a young woman, worked for Octavia Hill, and met Samuel Augustus Barnett (1844-1915) then 'a plain and insignificant curate'. After their marriage the Barnetts moved to St Jude's Parish, Whitechapel where they began their campaign against social and moral degradation.

In 1889 the Barnetts purchased Heath End House at Hampstead, which they renamed St Jude's Cottage. Their weekend retreat was far larger than its name suggested and required a substantial staff of East End women and girls, trained for domestic service by Mrs Moore, Henrietta Barnett's old nurse.

The 323 acre Wyldes estate had been owned by Eton College since 1531. The timber-framed farmhouse dates from the 17th century, and was altered and extended through the years. Unspoilt undulating land, subdivided into irregular fields by hedgerows lay to the north, with a further farmstead at Temple Fortune. When construction of the Northern Line appeared imminent, Henrietta Barnett began her campaign to protect 'Wyldes' and its environs. This photograph, c.1880, shows the original approach from North End.

A 1914 postcard shows the changes made through the conversion of the barn to a residential wing, with further extensions which can be seen in the hip-roofed block behind. Its farming days over, 'Wyldes' was now the home of Raymond Unwin, who planned Hampstead Garden Suburb, and his offices, where many of the individual buildings were designed.

Raymond Unwin (1863-1940) was a follower of William Morris, and had been secretary of the Manchester Branch of the Socialist League. Trained as an engineer in Derbyshire, he began practice with his brother-in-law, Barry Parker (1867-1947) in 1896, and came south in 1904 when their layout plan for Letchworth Garden City was accepted. Unwin, who as a youth in Oxford, had become acquainted with Canon Barnett, was appointed as early as 1905 to prepare the first layout for the new Garden Suburb.

Raymond Unwin's living room and study at 'Wyldes', 1923. The fitted furniture in the background was originally made for his office in Buxton and incorporates a desk and cabinet for his large collection of lantern slides. On the extreme right, Ethel, his wife, can just be seen on a tall ladderback chair. The rush matting was typical of a lifestyle that included vegetarianism and a quest for simplicity.

OF OLD THIS ROOF HAS SHELTERED
  MANY AND DIVERSE MEN:
FROM COLLINS THE KEEPER OF COWS,
  TO DICKENS OF FAMOUS PEN.

HERE CAME OLIVE SCHREINER,
  KROPOTKIN THE PIONEER,
LINNELL THE PAINTER TRUE,
  AND BLAKE THE MYSTIC SEER.

WYLDES STILL EXTENDS A WELCOME
  TO FOLK FROM EVERY CLIME,
AND SENDS YOU CORDIAL GREETINGS
  THIS HAPPY CHRISTMAS TIME.

From Ethel & Raymond Unwin
Wyldes
London N.W. 3.

'Wyldes' remained the Unwins home for many years. Raymond Unwin died in 1940 in the United States, the outbreak of war having prevented his return, but Ethel Unwin remained until her death in 1949. They appreciated the long historic association with writers, artists, philosophers, and Socialists, as shown in their Christmas card, drawn by their niece, Brynhild Parker, c.1925.

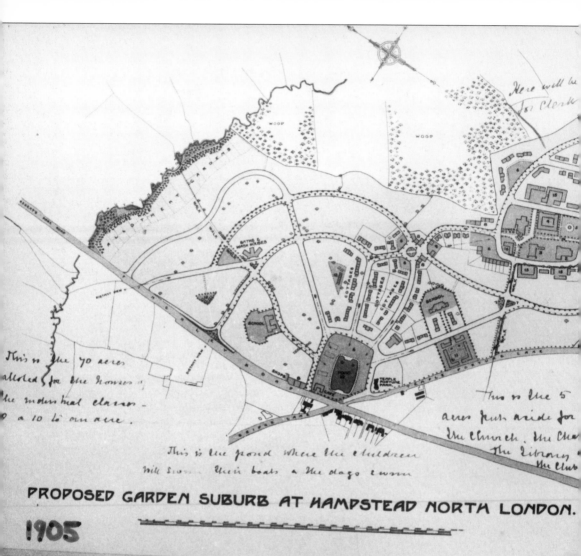

This is the 70 acres allotted for the houses of the industrial classes — @ a 10 to an acre.

This is the pond where the children will sail their boats & the dogs swim

This is the 5 acres put aside for the Church, the Chapel, the Library & the Club

Here will be for Clerk

**PROPOSED GARDEN SUBURB AT HAMPSTEAD NORTH LONDON.**

**1905**

The plan that pleased. Unwin's first plan for Hampstead Garden Suburb, dated 22 February 1905, was prepared to assist Henrietta Barnett's campaign to preserve the 80-acre Heath Extension, and develop its surroundings as a Garden Suburb for all classes. This copy includes her approving handwritten comments. The overall concept remained, but the road layout was made more formal, with the crowning Central Square later designed by Edwin Lutyens.

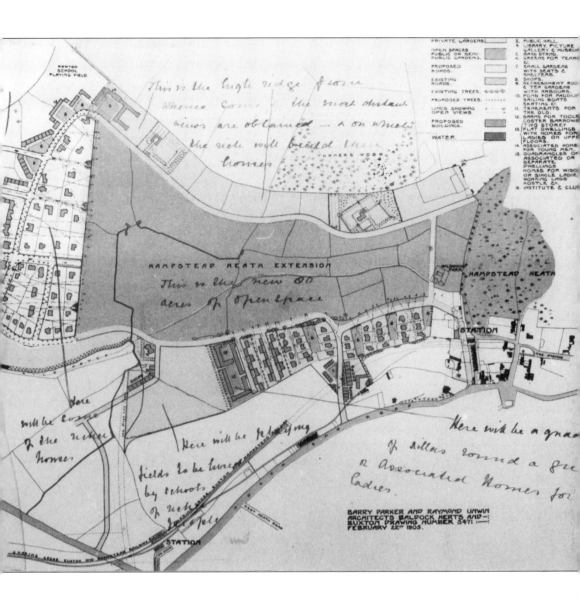

Turning the sod, 2 May 1907. Henrietta Barnett, centre, makes the first cut for the foundations of the 'Artisans' Quarter' at Temple Fortune, a development by Hampstead Tenants Ltd., a branch of the Co-Partners, a society interested in working-class housing. Behind her are Henry Vivian MP, Chairman of the Co-Partners, Alfred Lyttelton MP, Chairman of the Hampstead Garden Suburb Trust and Sir John Brunner MP, President of the Co-Partnership Tenants Housing Council. To the right of the central group stands Raymond Unwin, in a broad-brimmed trilby hat. In the background is the maypole around which children from the Co-Partners site at Ealing danced.

After the ceremony, the guests took lunch in a marquee erected in the 'pleasure gardens' of 'The Royal Oak', Finchley Road. No public houses were allowed in Hampstead Garden Suburb, but several well-known hostelries stood close by.

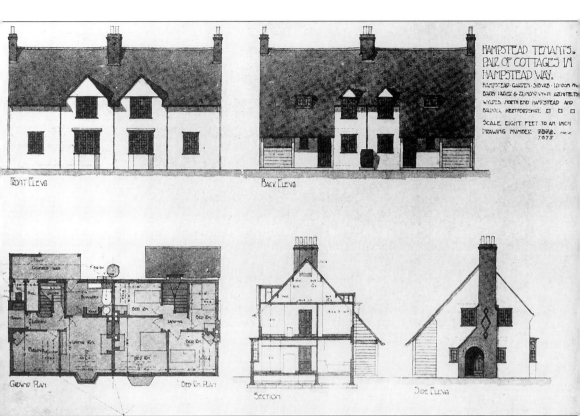

HAMPSTEAD TENANTS.
PAIR OF COTTAGES IN
HAMPSTEAD WAY.

HAMPSTEAD GARDEN SUBURB LONDON NW
BARRY PARKER & RAYMOND UNWIN ARCHITECTS
WYLDES NORTH END HAMPSTEAD AND
BALDOCK HERTFORDSHIRE □ □ □

SCALE EIGHT FEET TO AN INCH
DRAWING NUMBER 7372. MAX
7975

FRONT ELEVA          BACK ELEVA

GROUND PLAN          BED RM PLAN          SECTION          SIDE ELEVA

Plan by Barry Parker and Raymond Unwin for Nos 140-42 Hampstead Way, 'Foundation Cottages', the first to be built in the Garden Suburb. With his work at New Earswick, the Rowntree Garden Suburb outside York, Letchworth Garden City, and now Hampstead Garden Suburb, Raymond Unwin, and his talented staff, had now become expert in housing design. This pair, which still retains its original appearance, features a compact layout with four bedrooms, although the bath was originally located in the scullery on the ground floor, and the w.c. only accessible from the rear covered porches.

The Rev. Basil Bourchier with the Barnetts at Heath End House, 1909. The first Vicar of St Jude's, then under construction, Bourchier was characterised as a 'very handsome man, more like an actor than a clergyman', and does not seem entirely at ease with the Barnetts; he remained at St Jude's until 1930.

Henrietta laughs. It would be nice to know what prompted her and Canon Barnett to such unbridled mirth in the presence of the Prime Minister, Herbert Asquith, presenting them with a double portrait by Sir Hubert von Herkomer, in 1908.

After the opening of Queen Mary Hall at The Institute, Henrietta Barnett took Her Majesty up to the roof to look out over Bigwood Court and the land for 'the New Suburb', which was developed in the 1920s and 1930s. Lord Emmott completes the threesome.

Eminent octogenarians. Henrietta Barnett and the scientist and philosopher, Sir Oliver Lodge, were born within a month of each other. Here, in the old BBC Savoy Hill 2LO studios in 1931, they face the 'meat-safe' microphone used in the early days of broadcasting.

'Si monumentum requiris circumspice'. Although Dame Henrietta Barnett and Edwin Lutyens often quarrelled, the Hampstead Garden Suburb Trust chose him to design her memorial, appropriately located on the west side of Central Square facing her favourite view towards the distant prospect of Harrow Church. Mounted on Portland stone plinths, the elegant tracery of the bronze arches frame a view of the central block of The Institute, completed 1930. A miniature Cenotaph, topped with a carved laurel wreath, records Henrietta Barnett. The circular bed of heather has long since disappeared, as have the Lutyens' designed benches behind the memorial, which was unveiled in 1937.

# Two

# Around
# the 'Old Suburb'

Finchley Road - the Golders Green crossroads 1904. In the middle distance is the site of the future tube station. Although the Finchley Road, constructed in the 19th century, was a main turnpike out of London, its surface appears rutted and it is devoid of traffic. In the background can be seen the campanile and chapel of the Golders Green Crematorium, opened in 1902, designed by Sir Ernest George, and the most prominent local landmark until the construction of Hampstead Garden Suburb.

Golders Green Crematorium from the grounds, c.1910. The Crematorium site abuts Wild Hatch on the edge of the Suburb. The buildings front Hoop Lane which runs from the Meadway Gate towards the Finchley Road. Over the years, many Suburb residents, famous and unknown, have found a permanent commemoration in the cloisters which can be seen in front of the chapel.

24

Golders Green station, c.1910, 'the Hampstead Tube'. The new station was opened on Saturday 22 June 1907 by David Lloyd George, then President of the Board of Trade, and thousands of Londoners flocked up North End Road to the 'Old Bull and Bush' to enjoy refreshments and an illuminated open air concert. Charles Tyson Yerkes, the American promoter of the line, did not witness this success as he had died in New York in September 1905.

Around the corner from the railway station, the Suburb Trust constructed Rotherwick Road on land acquired from the Church Commissioners. A 'gateway' to the Suburb was formed by the buildings either side of the junction with the Finchley Road, one of which became the estate office. In the background the empty road stretches into the heart of the Suburb, construction of which has barely begun in this 1910 view.

Asmuns Place, 1907-08, Unwin's masterpiece of cottage design. This cul-de-sac of housing served to preserve the mature tree seen at the right, and street trees were planted which soon gave a verdant character to the road.

Hampstead Way looking up Asmuns Hill, about 1912. Nos 140-42 Hampstead Way, 'Foundation Cottages', stand left of the road junction. The gardens in the foreground were lost when Queens Court was built in 1928. This fine photograph, and many others in this section, are from an album of views of the Suburb, pre-1914, presented by Raymond Unwin to Henrietta Barnett. The glass negatives survive at Manchester University.

This view, from the tower on the Temple Fortune House, shows the central garden, which was planned to include a boating lake and paddling pool. In the middle distance are the contractor's huts, while the housing looks fresh and new. On the hill in the far background is the first phase of The Institute, but the construction of twin churches has yet to commence. The Big Wood crowns the horizon.

Looking back at Arcade House, it is evident that the design was carefully considered by A J Penty, working in Parker and Unwin's office, to present a good appearance from the gardens. The balcony at the rear of the building gives access to the flats above the shops, with a staircase to the garden below, which crosses on a bridge over the sunken service road - a remarkably modern piece of planning.

Builders' yard, Farm Walk and Hampstead Way, about 1909. William Moss and Sons were a Loughborough firm which successfully tendered for constructing much of the early housing in Hampstead Garden Suburb. Their yard occupies outbuildings of the old Temple Fortune farm, where purpose-designed casement windows, are stacked ready for use. In the distance a lady crosses the road pushing a perambulator, and there are horse-drawn delivery carts beyond.

# William Moss & Sons, L<sup>TD</sup>

## BUILDERS & CONTRACTORS

# Hampstead Way, Hendon

### REGISTERED OFFICES, LOUGHBOROUGH

ARE NOW BUILDING THE HOUSES ILLUSTRATED IN THIS BOOKLET, AS CONTRACTORS TO THE GARDEN SUBURB DEVELOPMENT COMPANY (HAMPSTEAD), LIMITED

## Some works executed by William Moss & Sons, Ltd.

| CONTRACTS | ENGINEERS OR ARCHITECTS | AMOUNTS |
|---|---|---|
| Uppingham Water Works, Rutland | Messrs. G. & F. W. Hodson, Westminster, S.W., and Loughborough | £15,000 |
| Ilkeston and Heanor Water Supply, Derbyshire | Messrs. G. & F. W. Hodson, Westminster, S.W., and Loughborough | £60,000 |
| Service Reservoir for Nottingham Corporation | W. B. Bryan, Esq., Buckhurst Hill, Essex | £13,000 |
| Covered Reservoir for Hull Corporation | F. J. Bancroft, Esq., A.M.I.C.E., Town Hall, Hull | £30,000 |
| Model Shoe Factory, Stafford | W. H. Simpson, Esq., Leicester | £60,000 |
| Extensions to Leicester Borough Asylum | Messrs. G. T. Hine & Co., Parliament Street, Westminster | £70,000 |
| Additions to Dorset County Asylum | Messrs. G. T. Hine & Co., Parliament Street, Westminster | £40,000 |
| Additions to Hill End Asylum, St. Albans (now in the course of construction) | Messrs. G. T. Hine & Co., Parliament Street, Westminster | £23,000 |
| Additions to Kent County Asylum | W. J. Jennings, Esq., Canterbury | £40,000 |
| New Workhouse Infirmary Leicester | Messrs. Giles, Gough & Trollope, Craven Street, Strand, W.C. | £100,000 |
| Leicester and Rutland Counties Asylum | Messrs. Everard, Son & Pick, Millstone Lane, Leicester | £180,000 |
| Messrs. Parrs New Bank, Leicester | Messrs. Everard, Son & Pick, Millstone Lane, Leicester | £45,000 |
| Schools at Gainsborough and Cleethorpes | Messrs. Scorer and Gamble, Lincoln | £24,000 |
| Furniture Factory at Colwick | W. B. Starr, Esq., Nottingham | £45,000 |

1

In 1908, William Moss and Sons Ltd proudly proclaimed their work in Hampstead Garden Suburb and elsewhere in this artistic advertisement in a promotional brochure, highlighting the achievement of 'Town Planning and Modern Architecture in the Hampstead Garden Suburb'.

In 1911-12 construction of further artisans' housing along Addison Way began. Here, the junction with Hogarth Hill is framed by hip-roofed towers, while the vista is stopped by the long terrace in the middle distance. This is one of the finest Parker and Unwin designed housing groups.

Addison Way was designed to accommodate working people, with flats renting from 5s 9d per week (29p). On the right of the picture, between the blocks, can be seen the landscaped setting of Mutton Brook which formed the northern boundary of the 'Old Suburb'.

'Crickmer Circus' was a housing grouping designed by Courtenay Crickmer from Letchworth, framing the junction of Temple Fortune Hill and Willifield Way. The bold double gables were characteristic of his work.

A short distance along Willified Way, 'Lucas Crescent', designed by Geoffry Lucas of Hitchin, preserved the existing trees by setting the housing back behind a communal green.

At the junction of Hampstead Way and Willifield Way there was originally an open green leading upwards into Central Square, with the twin churches, the Free Church (left) and St Jude's (right) dominating the skyline.

Looking south, the vista was stopped by the fine house in the middle distance designed by T. Laurence Dale. A smartly dressed lady on the seat appears lost in contemplation. The diagram in the bottom left hand corner shows how Unwin followed an example by the Austrian architect Camillo Sitte in arranging the buildings around the road junction.

Hill Close, looking very new in this 1913 view, leads upwards to North Square and the tower and newly completed spire of St Jude's provide a focal point.

Looking south along Hampstead Way, the junction with Meadway can be seen in the distance, is marked by the attractive picturesque gables of 'Baillie Scott Corner'. To see this familiar view with a total absence of traffic, or even people, creates an almost surreal atmosphere.

A closer view of the junction of Hampstead Way and Meadway shows the fine detailing of the Baillie Scott houses which turn the corner. The half-timbered gable is a genuine construction, not in timber strips fixed to solid brickwork as in so many later examples. In the far distance can be seen the tall chimneystack an idiosyncratic pair of houses designed by the architect Matthew Dawson.

On the north side of Meadway is a fine group of houses designed by the architect Michael Bunney, in one of which he lived himself. In this view, about 1910, they stand in glorious isolation, with the vacant site at the right waiting to receive the contrasting Georgian style houses designed by the Co-Partners' architect, G L Sutcliffe.

GOLDERS GREEN, MEADWAY GATE.

At its west end, Meadway sweeps around a central garden with landscaping and pergola before joining Hoop Lane. In the early years, as this photograph shows, it was a popular venue for nannies and nurses with their charges. At the right hand side, the gas lantern and cast-iron lamp post are typical of the period.

Heathgate, leading from Meadway to the Heath Extension, projects a vista from the transept of St Jude's to Sunshine Corner where it joins the Heath Extension. It is flanked by fine individual houses, that on the left designed by the architect Curtis Green. Vistas and gateways of the type shown on this page were a feature of planning in the Suburb.

35

Sometimes architects' drawings tended to exaggerate the size and spacing of the houses. No. 10 Southway, designed by Geoffry Lucas in 1909, appears to stand in glorious isolation, with a forest background, in this charming drawing which rather overstated its situation.

The fine house on the right was intended as one of a pair - the other never turned up. It was designed in 1910 by Guy Dawber and faces a driveway which gives a view through to the Heath Extension. In the middle distance is seen The Great Wall, with one of its gazebos, which divides the Suburb from the countryside beyond.

Between Linnell Drive and Meadway, Linnell Close presents a group of solid country Queen Anne style houses set round a central green. In this early view, quick growing creeper has almost colonised one of the houses, which evidently also suffers from problems with smoking chimneys. The architect for most of the group was Michael Bunney.

In 1912, The Great Wall looked very new indeed, as vegetation had not yet colonised it or its setting. It was designed and detailed by Charles Wade, an assistant of Unwin's, who later retired to the Cotswolds and created his own Arts and Crafts Utopia at Snowshill Manor.

Sunshine Corner is a broad terrace, with seats, raised to give a view south towards the Heath Extension. In this 1914 view, St Jude's, and Heathgate form a backdrop, with nannies and their charges taking advantage of the fine weather and the playground of the nearby Heath Extension.

The gazebos, as in this 1912 view, commanded fine views of the Heath Extension.

From a vantage point just below 'The Spaniards', there is an impressive prospect, of Hampstead Heath, the Heath Extension in the middle distance, with the Suburb beyond, crowned by the spire of St Jude's. This atmospheric view, taken in the 1920s has scarcely changed.

Guarding the corner of Hampstead Way and Corringham Road, this impressive angled block designed by Unwin, turns the corner, and has a charming Chinese Chippendale balcony to command views towards the Heath Extension. On the opposite corner, at the left of this 1914 photograph, the pleached trees have long since disappeared.

The Corringham Road Squares are set back either side of the road. Formal in design, influenced by Lutyens, although designed by Parker and Unwin, the front gardens were as this 1914 view shows originally closed off from the road by a fence, in position while the hedge was growing, and a small field gate.

Corringway, seen from Corringham Road, was originally developed as garages with chauffeurs' flats above. In 1912, a writer for *The Builder* trade journal wished to see 'a small inferno for motors only' so that the families living above the garages could be spared the effects of continuous motor traffic. How prophetic of a situation where the car has virtually taken over parts of the Suburb. The old flats were demolished recently, and new blocks are taking shape.

Rotherwick Road was the principal route from the tube station into the Suburb. It was lined by houses of a more urban character than elsewhere, including this fine semi-detached pair, designed in 1908 by Barry Parker in the Parker and Unwin office at Letchworth.

Other architects saw the merits of grouped housing designs. These substantial houses in Temple Fortune Lane were designed by Edwin Palser, and shared the impressive green in foreground.

*747. Lucas Square, Hampstead Garden Suburb.*

Lucas Square, off Hampstead Way, was designed by the versatile Geoffry Lucas and, likewise, featured a central green, with a small sundial, recently replaced in memory of the actor Cyril Luckham (1907-89), resident in the square.

*Waterloo Court, Hampstead Garden Suburb.*

Waterlow Court, designed by Baillie Scott, lay at the end of the contrasting Parker and Unwin-designed Heath Close. In this early postcard, the publisher misprinted the name as 'Waterloo'. A single bicycle leans against the temporary post and wire fence along the garden frontage - a contrast to the continuous kerbside parking of today.

Not far away, Reynolds Close was wholly designed by Parker and Unwin. About 1912, two intrepid lady motorists, complete with ankle length overcoats and veiled hats are about to be driven away in their limousine. A cyclist looks on admiringly. Clearly motor cars were objects of wonder before the First World War.

The Reynolds Close houses were linked by arches and first floor loggias. In this fine 1914 photograph the refinement of detail can be seen, together with the lovely, even if recently planted garden, which acts as a natural foil to the architecture.

Contrasts in the domestic architecture of Hampstead Way. In the foreground, No. 27 was designed by Herbert Welch in the Georgian style. It contrasts with 'Clere' on the distant corner of Wellgarth Road, designed by Barry Parker in 1914, a fine late Arts and Crafts house.

Parker and Unwin had written a book in 1901 called 'The Art of Building a Home'. These contrasting examples of their work aptly illustrate the title. The rear loggia of 'Clere' makes a positive connection with the garden, and is framed by a tile-creased arch. On the first floor above, a balcony with French windows reiterates the connection between indoors and out. Notice the golf bag and clubs casually leaning against the sheltered ground floor wall, with the blur of a small child outside the french doors who has evidently not remained still during the timed exposure.

Opposite: 'Boundary House' was designed in Unwin's Hampstead Office and is a superb example of a simple design relying for its effect on good materials and proportions. The house stands on the fringe of Hampstead Heath and on the edge of the Suburb itself. Climbing roses are already beginning to colonise the substantial pergola, while Alpines nestle between the rubble stones of the retaining walls of the stepped terraces.

*Three*

# Central Squares, Churches and Club House

Big Wood formed a natural backdrop to North Square and its approach from Erskine Hill. In this pre-1914 photograph, by T.R. Rodger, the winter woods have a light covering of snow, highlighting the silhouettes of the distant children.

In Spring and Summer the woods formed a verdant playground as shown in another Rodger photograph.

Edwin Lutyens was appointed in 1906 to plan the formal centre of the Suburb. His familiar plan of three linked squares, defined by the major public buildings, emerged in 1908-9. In this early 1930s aerial photograph, the twin churches, the Free Church (left) and St Jude (right), frame The Institute. At the top of the picture the fast growing 'New Suburb' extends along Northway, Middleway and Southway.

Erskine Hill, looking south, about 1911. The fine Georgian style houses by Lutyens on the west side lead the eye upwards to North Square and the Free Church, under construction. The road is still a muddy track.

A view from the scaffolding of the Free Church shows the east side of Erskine Hill is used as a builders' yard. Beyond are the roofs of Erskine Hill and Willifield Way, with the valley of Mutton Brook, now occupied by the North Circular Road, separating the Suburb from Finchley on the far hillside.

The group of houses on the west of North Square was fully designed by Lutyens. Characteristic touches include the two-toned brickwork, dominant chimneystacks, and the triumphal arch motif in the corner giving access to the rear gardens through the block. In this 1911 view, the buildings rise out of a sea of mud of the site for the Free Church.

South Square was not fully designed by Lutyens, but follows his style. Henrietta Barnett lived at No. 2 South Square, left; beyond are the then unfinished west ends of both churches, in this late 1920s photograph.

'God is larger than the Creeds'. Henrietta Barnett lays a foundation stone with an inscription which was approved by H M Queen Mary before the Elders of the Church were convinced of its appropriateness. The ceremony took place on 16 March 1911.

The parish church of St Jude-on-the-Hill was named after the Barnetts' church in the East End. Designed by Lutyens, Henrietta Barnett required several revisions before she was satisfied. By late 1910/early 1911, the nave, transepts and chancel were complete, with a temporary roof before the tower and spire was added. To the left is the newly completed Vicarage. The contractor came from Rugby, as his board indicates.

To contrast with St Jude's spire, Lutyens designed a dome to crown the crossing on the Free Church. In 1911, the elaborate wooden centring and scaffolding is in position for the construction of the crossing arches and inner dome.

The tower and spire of St Jude's under construction 1912-13. Henrietta Barnett wanted a Gothic silhouette for the new parish church, which Lutyens achieved without using any pointed arches or reproduction detail. The spire was constructed with money from a special fund commemorating Henrietta Barnett's fiftieth birthday and was completed in 1913.

The interior of St Jude's originally had plain whitewashed walls, highlighting the fine brickwork and Classical detailing of Lutyens's design. In the early 1920s, Basil Bourchier commissioned Walter Starmer to paint murals throughout.

On Christmas Day 1928, the church was dedicated by the Bishop of London, in the presence of HRH Princess Royal, free of the initial debt of construction costs. The Bishop (centre) with Bourchier (centre right) and Church Wardens pose outside the yet-to-be completed West End, while one of the PCC members proudly holds a model aloft.

Both churches organised a full range of social activities; here Bourchier's successor, Rev W.H. Maxwell Rennie, presides over a game of trains in the nave. In the background, apart from Starmer's murals, can be seen a memorial to horses slaughtered in the battles of the Western Front during the First World War.

The Free Church organised a keen Guide troop, here seen on a ramble in 1923.

Church Sports Days were often informal affairs as in this 1912 photograph.

After the fun and games, what better than tea in the splendid surroundings of the Hall of The Institute with its fine Lutyens-designed fireplace.

The Institute was one of Henrietta Barnett's favourite organisations. Children planted trees to commemorate the opening of The Institute Hall on 28 March 1909. Lutyens's original elevation was later refronted and the doors now open into a foyer

At the opening, Henrietta Barnett (centre right) presided with a group that included, left to right, Henry Vivian, J.S. Birkett, Edwin Lutyens, Herbert Marnham, Canon Barnett, herself, Raymond Unwin, and Frederick Litchfield.

The Institute, showing from Pictures by Mr. Cyril Farey, A.A.R.I.B.A., how the buildings designed by Sir Edwin Lutyens, R.A., F.R.I.B.A., and Mr. Charles Hanscombe, F.R.I.B.A., will look when they are erected.

The Institute buildings were completed in stages between 1909 and 1930. These drawings, published in 1928, illustrate the centre block, linking the two wings, with the exterior designed by Lutyens, and the overall plan by Charles Hanscombe, the Middlesex County architect. This block was completed in 1930.

Over the years, The Institute has served many generations of adult students. The art classes, many conducted in the temporary buildings that have surrounded The Institute, have attracted many well-known students, for relaxation. At the easel, centre left, is Patrick Gordon Walker, Foreign Secretary under Harold Wilson in the 1960s.

Sculpture class: Howard Bute, Institute sculptor 1953-71, discusses a model from life with one of his students.

The Club House on Willifield Green was strategically situated on the edge of the original 'Artisan's Quarter' and was intended to promote mixing between the social classes within the Suburb. The building, designed by Parker and Unwin, which included a main hall, and extensive facilities, faced the green and was dominated by a tall, hip-roofed, rather Germanic tower. Pre-1914, children enjoy an informal game of cricket on the green.

The view south-east from the tower of the Club House gave a splendid panorama, dominated by the dome of the Free Church and the spire of St Jude's. In this pre-1914 postcard view, only a single delivery van is visible in the middle distance.

The Club House boasted an extensive library, seen here, while its hall was used for debating and meetings of the 'Garden Suburb Parliament'.

Meals and non-alcoholic drinks, were available at reasonable prices, although the well-laid table in this early photograph appears to have been set up specially for the photographer.

*Four*

# Life in Our
# Garden Suburb

The Orchard, designed by Parker and Unwin, and opened in 1909, provided some of the first purpose-built housing for the elderly, following the introduction of old age pensions. At the opening, Frederick Litchfield, Henry Vivian, Mrs Harris Brown, Henrietta Barnett and Sybella Gurney, stand on the balcony, with a crowd of Suburb residents in the quadrangle below.

By the 1930s, The Orchard had mellowed into an almost rural state.

Among the first residents were Mr and Mrs James Hosgood; he had been a gunner at the Siege of Sebastapol in the Crimean War. King George V and Queen Mary met the Hosgoods on their visit in March 1911.

The facilities provided in The Orchard now seem very primitive. A typical kitchen, seen in 1971, shortly before demolition, shows a porcelain butler sink with cold tap only, and a small gas stove adjoining. Regrettably, the Co-Partners who had developed the flats failed to keep them up to date or even to repair them.

Waterlow Court, designed by M.H. Baillie Scott in 1909, provided flats for business women.
H M Queen Mary emerges after a visit in March 1911, watched by Henry Vivian.

The flats at Waterlow Court faced a secluded quadrangle reminiscent of a traditional Oxbridge
college, with a cloistered walk on the ground floor, and staircase access to the flats.

Meals at Waterlow Court could be taken in this splendid Arts and Crafts style dining room, with its beamed ceiling and inglenook fireplace.

Individual flats were adaptable to home comforts by the residents as this interior view, pre-1914, of a second floor flat indicates.

Royal visits were regular events pre-First World War. Here King George V, with umbrella, accompanied by Henry Vivian who obscures Queen Mary, emerges from his visit to The Orchard on 18 March 1911.

Queen Mary, with the Prince of Wales (later King Edward VIII) and Princess Mary, opened the Barnett homestead, built in memory of Canon Barnett, on 26 February 1918. Henrietta Barnett stands to the left of the Royal visitors.

The houses in Denman Drive were amongst the first to be built in the 'New Suburb'. In 1915, the residents of No 44 entertain visitors in their newly planted garden.

Is the view from the window intriguing, or are the ladies just smiling for the photographer? Sunday-best dress, including hats, was the order of the day for such visits.

The back gardens, and allotment plots, soon became both aesthetically pleasing and productive as this view of the backs of houses in Hampstead Way (left) and Temple Fortune Lane (right) shows.

Gardening became one of the most popular forms of recreation. Here, the proud resident of 144 Hampstead Way tends her verdant herbaceous bed.

The Hampstead Garden Suburb Horticultural Society was formed in 1909, and their exhibitions soon became annual events. A veritable cornucopia of flowers and produce are on display, pre-1923, in The Institute Hall.

To celebrate the 80th birthday of the Horticultural Society, 'Gardeners' Question Time' came to the Suburb on 29 January 1989. Sue Philips, Stefan Buczacki, Clay Jones, Norman Wheatley and Fred Downham receive a posy from young Jacqueline Murrell.

In its traffic-free early years the Suburb was an idyllic place for children, as this joyful group of girls, running along the middle of Willifield Way, indicates.

Clearly ready to grace any major event, these young girls line up their floral-decorated tricycles outside The Institute, c.1930.

A group of children in one of the Asmuns Place play-houses pre-First World War. These charming gazebos were damaged during the Second World War and were later demolished.

Children were introduced to gardening at an early age. Here, the Childrens' Garden Association, run by the Club House, tend their plots behind Addison Way and Wordsworth Walk.

'Mens sana in corpore sano' was surely a motto underlying many of the activities in the Suburb. Here a health group, including toddlers, prepares for exercise on the tennis court behind the Club House.

The Leas Lodge School, run by Miss Mulliner in Kingsley Way, is fondly remembered by many older Suburb residents. In 1936, she, and her young pupils go through their 'daily dozen' prior to classes.

The Garden Suburb School in Childs Way was opened in 1913; one of the early infant classes concentrate on building towers with the wooden precursor of 'Lego'.

In a similar classroom, a girls' class of 1923 displays their written work. Many children in the Suburb received private education and the 1000 pupil school was only half occupied in the late 1920s.

The Wellgarth Road Nursery Training School opened in 1915, during the First World War. Its imposing building with broad balconies and sliding windows to encourage fresh-air circulation, is now occupied by the Youth Hostels Association.

In 1934, the Warden, Miss Talbot, who ran the school from 1924-47, poses with her staff and their infant charges, orphans from the East End.

The Hampstead Tenants Social Council organised a Sports Day on the Recreation Ground off Meadway in September 1913; there was an exciting finish to the mens' sprint.

Womens events were generally less hectic; the winner of the egg and spoon race is rapt in concentration as she nears the finishing tape.

Suburb milkman with handcart, churn, pail and cans, from the Garden Suburb Dairy at Golders Green, c.1910.

As his advert promised, J. Morgan provided locally produced milk, butter and fresh farm eggs, with three daily deliveries.

Local grocers were soon established on the fringes of the Garden Suburb. At Temple Fortune, the Garden Suburb Supply Association shows its well-stocked windows, replete with enormous pyramids of goods, while outside, the customers' bycles, and delivery handcart are casually placed.

Construction of the Market Place on Addison (later Falloden) Way began in 1914. Mrs Kemp opened one of the earliest shops, with confectionery, tobacco, general goods and a tea room: she poses with her daughter and her dog, Master Jack Streeton.

**GENTILITY IN OUR GARDEN SUBURB.**

"Just think of it, Mrs. Brown has got the telephone fixed. I wouldn't have one."
"Why not?" "You have to associate with anybody."

The *Punch* artist, F.H. Townsend, moved into Hampstead Garden Suburb in 1911, and until his death in 1920, published a series of gently satirical sketches on the them of 'life in our Garden Suburb'. In this 1913 example, the social difficulties of the telephone, in the absence of a servant to answer it, are underlined, with a background which shows Meadway.

*Our Win-the-War Garden Suburb Enthusiast (as the storm bursts).* "Madam! Madam! Will you kindly put down your umbrella? It's keeping the rain off my allotment."

As in the Second World War, cultivation of allotments for produce was an important activity on the home front. This altercation is taking place on the allotments between Temple Fortune Hill and Hampstead Way, with a distant glimpse of St Jude's spire.

The Friends Meeting House on North Square, was designed by Fred Rowntree in 1913 and modelled on Jordans, Pennsylvania, a delightful building nestling serenely below North Square, as if consciously avoiding the pomp and circumstance of Lutyens's architecture.

The Tea House in Northway was run by the Hampstead Garden Suburb Trust, and was a popular venue for refreshments for visitors and users of the nearby Institute.

The opening of the first cottage in the Suburb on 9 October 1907 by Sir William Treloar, Lord Mayor of London, was long celebrated. Here, a 'Treloar Day Pagent' assembles in front of The Institute Hall.

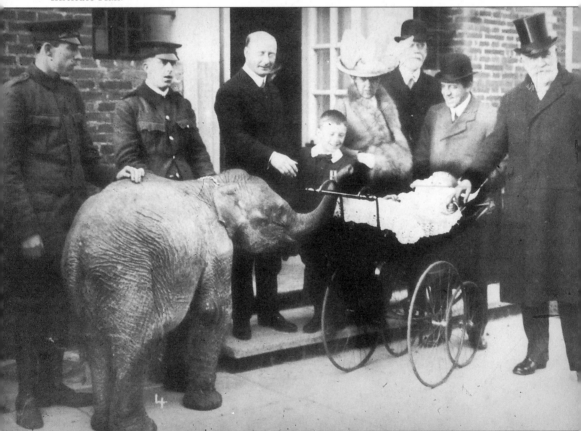

Events on 'Treloar Day' in 1912 were somewhat bizarre. Sir Frederick Litchfield and others welcome a baby elephant to The Suburb, brought by his keepers to the steps of The Institute, and about to take hold of the perambulator handle with his trunk.

**The JUNE MASQUE**
*By PAUL JEWITT*
HAMPSTEAD · GARDEN · SUBURB
JUNE 21st & 28th AT 3:30 & 6:30 P.M.

Masques and pageants were a feature of community life before the First World War. Paul Jewitt was a local school master who wrote a series of plays for outdoor performance. The June masque was given on the old pageant ground near Big Wood.

The Masque of Fairthorpe was presented in 1910. The plot was an allegory, representing the saving of the fairest countryside from the onslaught of Jerry builders by the Suburb Trust, and its enhancement by horticulture. Besmocked, carrying the implements of their trade, with a backdrop of Big Wood the gardeners sang:

> 'And he that will our pleasure share
> Let him come breath our coutry air;
> He'll find no better anywhere, ...
> ... And who would see a picture fair
> Should scan the view from Central Square;
> He'll find no better anywhere!

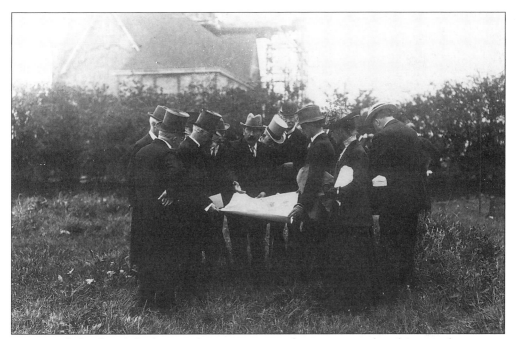

Hampstead Garden Suburb soon became renowned as an example of 'town planning in practice'. In 1912, Henry Vivian and Raymond Unwin, display a plan of the 'New Suburb' to visiting MP's. Behind the hedge, the tower of St Jude's is under construction.

International visits were frequent before the First World War. Henry Vivian, with a young girl on his knee, sits in the centre of an enthusiastic group of German town planners, posed in Asmuns Place, on their visit in 1912.

## The Garden City Method of Development.

FRONT GARDENS TO HOUSES UNDER TOWN PLANNING.

## The By-Law Method of Development.

ORDINARY SUBURBAN VILLAS, SHOWING AMOUNT OF SPACE FOR FRONT GARDEN.

'Nothing gained by overcrowding' was the message given by Unwin's town planning tract of 1912. The contrast between the lush arcadia of Hampstead Garden Suburb shown by a view of gardens in Hampstead Way, and the monotony of Victorian By-law housing was underscored in these paired photographs.

*Five*

# Two Wars...
# and Between

Recreation Room. The Garden Suburb Auxiliary Military Hospital, Willifield Way, N.W

With the addition of temporary wooden wards, the Club House on Willifield Green served as an auxillary military hospital during the First World War. Here soldiers recuperate with billiards, cards, a piano and, in the background, a large horn gramophone.

Home Leave. This young soldier stands with his family outside the entrance to Meadway Court in 1916. It is to be hoped that he returned safely home after the 1918 Armistice.

Development of the 'New Suburb' got under way in the interwar period. Bigwood Court, originally designed as 'flats for officers' families' included well maintained tennis courts.

Brookland Rise branched off Addison Way, and was developed in the mid-1920s just as Falloden Way was under construction to link to the new Barnet By-pass at Hendon Way. Although the houses nearest the camera have been completed, scaffolding, building materials and contractors signboards are visible in the distance.

Eastholm also dates from the 1920s, one of the culs-de-sac off Addison (Falloden) Way. The road has not yet been surfaced, and contractors are about to begin work on the terrace at the top of the hill.

This view shows the completed block at the head of Eastholm about two years later. The telegraph pole indicates the spread of telephone services to even the smallest homes in the Suburb.

Flats became popular in the 1930s. Belvedere Court, Lyttelton Road, designed by Ernst Freud (son of the great psycho-analyst) in 1935, is one of the finest examples, with its streamlined bays, influenced by the work of such Continental architects as Eric Mendelsohn.

The new flats incorporated the latest kitchens. This example, fully tiled and fitted is taken from 'The Pantiles', constructed on the Finchley Road in 1934, and was published in a book promoting 'Ascot' gas water heaters.

Although the Market Place had been begun before the First World War, its development was not finished until after the Falloden Way-Lyttelton Road link had been been completed in the mid 1920s. This view, about 1925, shows the fine vista along Northway towards The Institute, screened by later development.

In the early 1930s, a lone 'Austin Chummy' is parked at the kerbside, with the newly completed and partly occupied block of shops and flats in the background.

The expedient upgrading of Falloden Way by the Ministry of Transport in 1926 has caused traffic and severance problems ever since. This photograph shows the calm before the storm. The road has not yet been fully metalled, and the lone car parked against the kerbside gives no hint of the future deluge of traffic.

Only a few years later, traffic conditions resulted in local protests. In 1937, the Rev. Maxwell Rennie, of St Jude's Church, leads a demonstration to demand a 30 mph speed limit.

Temple Fortune consolidated its position as the shopping centre for the west of the Suburb in the interwar period. The fine Parker and Unwin buildings, Arcade House and Temple Fortune House, were joined by later parades along the Finchley Road. Looking south, in 1929, the main route into West End London appears remarkably traffic-free compared with today.

Looking north, a tramcar ambles down the centre of the road, with pedestrians walking out to board it. Kerbside parking is still remarkably light.

The cinema became the most popular form of mass entertainment in the 1920s. The Orpheum was built on Garden Suburb land, most probably against Henrietta Barnett's better judgement. Its Babylonian splendour was designed by Yates, Cook and Darbyshire, and this 'super talkie palace' opened on Saturday 11 October 1930. Its first programme featured 'Condemned' starring Ronald Colman, and a stage show with twenty five dancing girls.

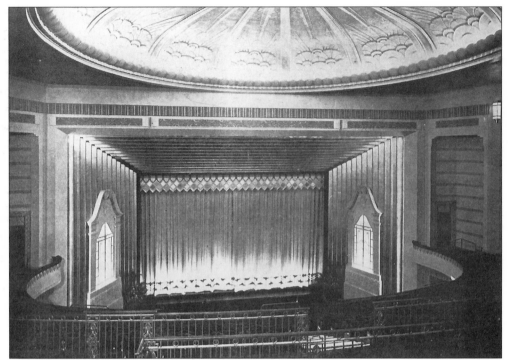

The vast fan-shaped auditorium of The Orpheum was designed to reflect the sound of the talkies to the furthest seat. During the intermission, the audience was entertained by the latest Compton organ complete with percussion and a set of cathedral chimes.

Before and after the show, tea and light refreshments could be taken in the lounge, with its jazz-patterned carpet and comfortable Lloyd Loom chairs. Prices of admission ranged from 1s.0d to 3s.6d (5p-17 Q w p) - what value!

Suburb groups produced their own theatrical entertainment. Here the HGS Operatic Society parade to publicise their forthcoming production of Gilbert and Sullivan's 'The Yeomen of the Guard', in 1926.

UNLOADING ARTS LEAGUE OF SERVICE TRAVELLING THEATRE    THE ARTS LEAGUE OF SERVICE
1 ROBERT STREET, ADELPHI, LONDON

Henrietta Barnett had hoped to establish a permanent theatre in the Suburb. Her endeavours were not realised, but visiting groups often used The Institute Hall: in the late 1920s, the Arts League of Service Travelling Theatre unload their props.

Royal occasions continued through the interwar years. In June 1931, HRH Duchess of York (now H M Queen Elizabeth the Queen Mother) arrives at The Institute to meet Henrietta Barnett and accompany her to a pageant in Little Wood.

Seated before the performance, the Duchess is flanked by Henrietta Barnett and John Garside.

The cast of the revival of Adam Bell, which was given before the Duchess. In the centre, the King was played by Gilbert Walsh, and the Queen by Tobes Coffin.

Hampstead Garden Suburb has been home to many famous personalities. The actor, Robert Donat (1905-58) lived at 8 Meadway in the 1930s, the period when his greatest film successes included The 39 Steps and Goodbye Mr Chips.

Dame Myra Hess (1890-1965), one of the most musical pianists, famed for her war time National Gallery concerts, was resident at 48 Wildwood Road until her death.

Politics has produced many eminent residents of Hampstead Garden Suburb. Margaret Bondfield (1873-1953) was the first woman Cabinet Minister and held the Labour portfolio 1929-31 in Ramsay MacDonald's Labour administration. Miss Bondfield was also the first woman chairman of the General Council of the Trades Union Congress. She lived in Denman Drive in the 1930s.

Harold Wilson (1916-95) was Prime Minister 1964-70 and 1974-77, and moved from Southway to Downing Street.

Norrice Lea Synagogue was built in 1934 to serve the Jewish population in the rapidly expanding 'new Suburb'. It was built on land donated by the builder, H Meckhonik, and designed by the architect Maurice de Metz. The building was officially opened on 22 September 1935. This interior view shows the pulpit and ark shortly after opening.

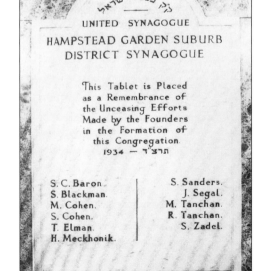

A tablet in the vestibule records the efforts of the Founders to form the Congregation of the Synagogue.

Parade of ARP and Guides in Central Square, June 1940, reviewed by M. Naar, Mayor of Hendon.

'Doing their bit', the ARP parade past St Jude's Vicarage in July 1941, commemorating a visit from the Bishop of London.

The Club House on Willifield Green fell victim to aerial assault on 25 September 1940. Its front was blown off, and the tower was fatally cracked. It was demolished and replaced by Fellowship House.

Opposite, 119-123 Willifield Way were shattered ruins the morning after the same raid.

The 'New Suburb' took its share of destruction. This house on the corner of Brim Hill and Gurney Drive had its front blown off, and looks like a wrecked dolls house.

Nearby, 63 and 65 Brookland Rise disappeared under a pile of rubble on 1 October 1940.

Studiously working in class, the girls of the Henrietta Barnett Junior School display their 'grow more food' and 'dig for victory' posters on the notice board.

After the war, the tunic and gymslip image was abandoned and satirised by these girls, posing as inmates of St Trinians at the 1957 Golden Jubilee Parade.

Although just outside the Suburb, the King Alfred School, which moved to Manor Wood, North End Road in 1920, educated many Suburb children in a liberal co-educational atmosphere. The buildings were designed by Barry Parker, and this photograph shows the library block in 1932, shortly after completion.

Open-air education was a feature of the school, and the class here is working in 'Squirrel Hall', whose roof is supported by the branches of a fine old tree.

The King Alfred School was requisitioned by the War Office and re-opened in September 1945. The children played their part in refurbishing the buildings: in this 1945-6 view, Alister Pease, Anne Fielding, Lorna Lea and Gillian Pugh are hard at work.

*Six*

# Commemoration
# and Change

In 1957, the Suburb celebrated its Golden Jubilee. In July, HRH Princess Margaret visited and toured the area, accompanied by Sir John Braithwaite, President of the Golden Jubilee Committee.

History repeats itself. The Lord Mayor of London, Sir Cullum Welch, visits No 142 Hampstead Way, and meets the then resident, Mrs McCarthy, fifty years after his predessor Sir William Treloar had seen the first cottages to be completed.

The Jubilee Committee organised a full programme of events and the motif, showing the skyline of the Central Square buildings, was later used as the Residents' Association logo.

*HAMPSTEAD GARDEN SUBURB JUBILEE*

1907   1957

*Souvenir Booklet and Programme*
*June 29 - July 6*

2s.

# HAMPSTEAD GARDEN SUBURB
# PROTECTION SOCIETY

---

## THE FIRST

# MEMBERS' MEETING

### WILL BE AT

# THE INSTITUTE

## CENTRAL SQUARE, N.W.11

### ON

# THURSDAY, APRIL 12TH, 1962

### AT

# 8 P.M.

During the 1960s, speculation and land transactions resulted in a Protection Society being convened to ensure that the Suburb did not lose its distinctive character. Eventually, the Protection Society negotiated for the reconstitution of the Hampstead Garden Suburb Trust.

In 1969, the freehold of much of the Suburb was sold by Suburb Leaseholds to the property company, Ashdale. The sale catalogue illustrated many of the distinctive houses and commercial buildings in the Suburb.

Matters had settled down by the time the Suburb celebrated its 70th Birthday in 1977. Brigid Grafton Green, long-time Suburb Archivist, who died in 1991, poses with copies of her commemorative history, published to celebrate the occasion.

Tree-planting was an almost ubiquitous commemorative activity, albeit that some of the species did not survive long. Here, on a cold May afternoon in 1977, the Residents' Association plant their offering in the grounds of the Henrietta Barnett School.

114

On 5 July 1979, the Queen Mother returned to the Suburb to visit gardens in Asmuns Hill and Westholm.

To celebrate the Suburb's 80th birthday, Mary Lutyens wields Henrietta Barnett's trusty spade to plant a commemorative tree in the shadow of St Jude's Church, arguably her father's masterpiece among the Central Square buildings.

The 75th Anniversary of founding the Suburb was marked by installing a Blue Plaque at Heath End House, where Henrietta and Samuel Barnett had lived when she began her campaign to protect the Heath Extension and build the Suburb. On 2 May 1982, Vera Gilchrist Thompson, Dame Geraldine Ayers and the Mayor of Barnet, Rosa Freedman stand in front of the newly unveiled plaque.

Around the Suburb, Blue Plaques proliferated commemorating the great and the good. In May 1992, Patricia Hayes and Ernie Wise unveiled a plaque to the comedian Tony Hancock, commemorating his short sojourn in Grey Close. The GLC had disbanded and the plaque was provided by the Dead Comics Society.

Motorised Anarchy: traffic continued to pour along Falloden Way in increasing intensity. Fortunately, a plan to widen the road to six lanes was resisted, but the issue has never been fully resolved. This photograph from the early 1970s vividly illustrates the incompatibility of heavy traffic with the domestic environment of the 'New Suburb'.

Jugger off! The proposed lorry route designation brought renewed protests. Tireless campaigner Terry Rand, and his family, participate in a protest in the Market Place in 1975.

If only .... Falloden Way was closed to traffic on 21 November 1982. Taking advantage of the respite, children cycle and roller skate down the highway, normally traffic-choked.

Window on the Suburb. Hampstead Garden Suburb was designated as a Conservation Area by the London Borough of Barnet in December 1968. The same year, the reconstituted Hampstead Garden Suburb Trust began to operate strong conservation controls as ground landlord. This early 1970s view from a cottage, indicates the special character which the Local Authority and Trust have an obligation to preserve or enhance.

Despite the traffic, a village-like character prevails throughout much of the Suburb. Individual tradesmen still operate door-to-door. In 1993, Laurence North, greengrocer, retired, after having risen at 3 am to bring fresh vegetables to the Suburb since 1946, after demobilisation following his regiment's return from Burma.

The knife-grinder pedals his way through the Suburb to maintain the culinary equipment and garden tools of residents.

In 1990, the Residents' Association, began to honour those who had made outstanding contributions to the Suburb and its life. Jean Henderson was one of England's first female barristers and was resident in the Suburb for many years before being drawn into the protection campaign in December 1961, by her friend George Bower. In the lengthy discussions to reconstitute the Trust, Miss Henderson's keen analytical mind was an indispensable asset.

John de Enderby served as Principal of The Institute from 1954 until his retirement thirty years later. In this photograph, the then Chairman of the Residents' Association, Tony Mandelson, presents John and his wife with a framed watercolour of a scene in the Suburb.

Although MP for the neighbouring constituency, East Finchley, Margaret Thatcher was no stranger to the Suburb. On 23 May 1973, as Secretary of State for Education and Science, she attended the Silver Jubilee Dinner of the Kerem Schools. She is seen here with the Chief Rabbi Jacobovits and Mr Stanley Frankfurt.

In 1983, as Prime Minister, Mrs Thatcher opened Birnbeck Court, elderly persons' housing on the site of the former Odeon (Orpheum) on the Finchley Road. Here she is deep in conversation with Christopher Kellerman, Manager of the Hampstead Garden Suburb Trust, while Tony Mandelson, then Residents' Association Chairman, looks on nonplussed.

Birnbeck Court involved a High Court battle which upheld the Trust's right to impose appropriate design standards for new developments. The overall concept included a tower reminiscent of the former Club House on Willifield Green.

In 1989, the Hampstead Garden Suburb Trust purchased the freehold held by Ashdale. In the Trust Office, in front of one of Unwin's early plans of the Suburb, are, left to right, Christopher Kellerman, Trust Manager, Gerry Mansell, then Trust Chairman, and R L Vigars of Ashdale.

Environment Week was introduced in the 1980s, to promote clean-up campaigns by residents. In 1988, Donald Sinden, Anne Saunders and Ernest Howey appeared to have found something particularly nasty in the bushes of Temple Fortune Lane.

Tony Mandelson, RA Chairman died suddenly in 1990. The following year, a seat in his memory was constructed on Willifield Green. On 11 May 1991, Cllr Roy Schutz praises a friend of the Suburb, watched by Mary and Peter Mandelson.

In 1989, in connection with the declaration of a 'litter-free zone', Virginia Bottomley, then a Junior Environment Minister, visits Asmuns Place, and is presented with a posy by Eleanor and Hugo Gaskell-Taylor, while the constituency MP, John Marshall, and Eileen Whelan, Residents' Association Chairman, look on. In the Summer 1995 Cabinet reshuffle, Mrs Bottomley took over the Department of National Heritage, and through it responsibility for protecting the historic buildings in the Suburb.

After suffering vandalism, and the indignity of a galvanised steel security fence, the Henrietta Barnett Memorial in Central Square was restored and rededicated in October 1990. Encouraged by Eileen Whelan (right) and John Marshall (centre right), Cllr Roy Schutz, Mayor of Barnet, performs the ceremony.

Following the event, police keep a vigilant eye on the elegant restored bronze arches.

The History Men. Stuart Gray, doyen of Suburb historians, and Mervyn Miller stand in front of the Great Wall in 1992, in connection with their joint book on the history of Hampstead Garden Suburb. Happily, Stuart Gray's 90th birthday was commemorated in June 1995 by a special tea at the Trust office.

Pressure for development and road-widening continues to affect the character of the Suburb and its setting. The Mutton Brook Valley, which forms a buffer zone to the north of the Suburb was identified as a valuable ecological survival at the long-running Public Inquiry into the construction of a tunnel on the A1-North Circular junction. Regrettably, this did not prevent the Minister from approving the scheme, and this tranquil scene will soon be part of Suburb history.

# Stock List

(Titles are listed according to the pre-1974 county boundaries)

## BERKSHIRE

**Wantage**
*Irene Hancock*
ISBN 0-7524-0146 7

## CARDIGANSHIRE

**Aberaeron and Mid Ceredigion**
*William Howells*
ISBN 0-7524-0106-8

## CHESHIRE

**Ashton-under-Lyne and Mossley**
*Alice Lock*
ISBN 0-7524-0164-5

**Around Bebington**
*Pat O'Brien*
ISBN 0-7524-0121-1

**Crewe**
*Brian Edge*
ISBN 0-7524-0052-5

**Frodsham and Helsby**
*Frodsham and District Local History Group*
ISBN 0-7524-0161-0

**Macclesfield Silk**
*Moira Stevenson and Louanne Collins*
ISBN 0-7524-0315 X

**Marple**
*Steve Cliffe*
ISBN 0-7524-0316-8

**Runcorn**
*Bert Starkey*
ISBN 0-7524-0025-8

**Warrington**
*Janice Hayes*
ISBN 0-7524-0040-1

**West Kirby to Hoylake**
*Jim O'Neil*
ISBN 0-7524-0024-X

**Widnes**
*Anne Hall and the Widnes Historical Society*
ISBN 0-7524-0117-3

## CORNWALL

**Padstow**
*Malcolm McCarthy*
ISBN 0-7524-0033-9

**St Ives Bay**
*Jonathan Holmes*
ISBN 0-7524-0186-6

## COUNTY DURHAM

**Bishop Auckland**
*John Land*
ISBN 0-7524-0312-5

**Around Shildon**
*Vera Chapman*
ISBN 0-7524-0115-7

## CUMBERLAND

**Carlisle**
*Dennis Perriam*
ISBN 0-7524-0166-1

## DERBYSHIRE

**Around Alfreton**
*Alfreton and District Heritage Trust*
ISBN 0-7524-0041-X

**Barlborough, Clowne, Creswell and Whitwell**
*Les Yaw*
ISBN 0-7524-0031-2

**Around Bolsover**
*Bernard Haigh*
ISBN 0-7524-0021-5

**Around Derby**
*Alan Champion and Mark Edworthy*
ISBN 0-7524-0020-7

**Long Eaton**
*John Barker*
ISBN 0-7524-0110-6

**Ripley and Codnor**
*David Buxton*
ISBN 0-7524-0042-8

**Shirebrook**
*Geoff Sadler*
ISBN 0-7524-0028-2

**Shirebrook: A Second Selection**
*Geoff Sadler*
ISBN 0-7524-0317-6

## DEVON

**Brixham**
Ted Gosling and Lyn Marshall
ISBN 0-7524-0037-1

**Around Honiton**
*Les Berry and Gerald Gosling*
ISBN 0-7524-0175-0

**Around Newton Abbot**
*Les Berry and Gerald Gosling*
ISBN 0-7524-0027-4

**Around Ottery St Mary**
*Gerald Gosling and Peter Harris*
ISBN 0-7524-0030-4

**Around Sidmouth**
*Les Berry and Gerald Gosling*
ISBN 0-7524-0137-8

## DORSET

**Around Uplyme and Lyme Regis**
*Les Berry and Gerald Gosling*
ISBN 0-7524-0044-4

## ESSEX

**Braintree and Bocking**
*John and Sandra Adlam and Mark Charlton*
ISBN 0-7524-0129-7

**Ilford**
*Ian Dowling and Nick Harris*
ISBN 0-7524-0050-9

**Ilford: A Second Selection**
*Ian Dowling and Nick Harris*
ISBN 0-7524-0320-6

**Saffron Walden**
*Jean Gumbrell*
ISBN 0-7524-0176-9

## GLAMORGAN

**Around Bridgend**
*Simon Eckley*
ISBN 0-7524-0189-0

**Caerphilly**
*Simon Eckley*
ISBN 0-7524-0194-7

**Around Kenfig Hill and Pyle**
*Keith Morgan*
ISBN 0-7524-0314-1

**The County Borough of Merthyr Tydfil**
*Carolyn Jacob, Stephen Done and Simon Eckley*
ISBN 0-7524-0012-6

**Mountain Ash, Penrhiwceiber and Abercynon**
*Bernard Baldwin and Harry Rogers*
ISBN 0-7524-0114-9

**Pontypridd**
*Simon Eckley*
ISBN 0-7524-0017-7

**Rhondda**
*Simon Eckley and Emrys Jenkins*
ISBN 0-7524-0028-2

**Rhondda: A Second Selection**
*Simon Eckley and Emrys Jenkins*
ISBN 0-7524-0308-7

**Roath, Splott, and Adamsdown**
*Roath Local History Society*
ISBN 0-7524-0199-8

## GLOUCESTERSHIRE

**Barnwood, Hucclecote and Brockworth**
*Alan Sutton*
ISBN 0-7524-0000-2

**Forest to Severn**
*Humphrey Phelps*
ISBN 0-7524-0008-8

**Filton and the Flying Machine**
*Malcolm Hall*
ISBN 0-7524-0171-8

**Gloster Aircraft Company**
*Derek James*
ISBN 0-7524-0038-X

**The City of Gloucester**
*Jill Voyce*
ISBN 0-7524-0306-0

**Around Nailsworth and Minchinhampton from the Conway Collection**
*Howard Beard*
ISBN 0-7524-0048-7

**Around Newent**
*Tim Ward*
ISBN 0-7524-0003-7

**Stroud: Five Stroud Photographers**
*Howard Beard, Peter Harris and Wilf Merrett*
ISBN 0-7524-0305-2

## HAMPSHIRE

**Gosport**
*Ian Edelman*
ISBN 0-7524-0300-1

**Winchester from the Sollars Collection**
*John Brimfield*
ISBN 0-7524-0173-4

## HEREFORDSHIRE

**Ross-on-Wye**
*Tom Rigby and Alan Sutton*
ISBN 0-7524-0002-9

## HERTFORDSHIRE

**Buntingford**
*Philip Plumb*
ISBN 0-7524-0170-X

**Hampstead Garden Suburb**
*Mervyn Miller*
ISBN 0-7524-0319-2

**Hemel Hempstead**
*Eve Davis*
ISBN 0-7524-0167-X

**Letchworth**
*Mervyn Miller*
ISBN 0-7524-0318-4

**Welwyn Garden City**
*Angela Eserin*
ISBN 0-7524-0133-5

## KENT

**Hythe**
*Joy Melville and Angela Lewis-Johnson*
ISBN 0-7524-0169-6

**North Thanet Coast**
*Alan Kay*
ISBN 0-7524-0112-2

**Shorts Aircraft**
*Mike Hooks*
ISBN 0-7524-0193-9

## LANCASHIRE

**Lancaster and the Lune Valley**
*Robert Alston*
ISBN 0-7524-0015-0

**Morecambe Bay**
*Robert Alston*
ISBN 0-7524-0163-7

**Manchester**
*Peter Stewart*
ISBN 0-7524-0103-3

## LINCOLNSHIRE

**Louth**
*David Cuppleditch*
ISBN 0-7524-0172-6

**Stamford**
*David Gerard*
ISBN 0-7524-0309-5

## LONDON
(Greater London and Middlesex)

**Battersea and Clapham**
*Patrick Loobey*
ISBN 0-7524-0010-X

**Canning Town**
*Howard Bloch and Nick Harris*
ISBN 0-7524-0057-6

**Chiswick**
*Carolyn and Peter Hammond*
ISBN 0-7524-0001-0

**Forest Gate**
*Nick Harris and Dorcas Sanders*
ISBN 0-7524-0049-5

**Greenwich**
*Barbara Ludlow*
ISBN 0-7524-0045-2

**Highgate and Muswell Hill**
*Joan Schwitzer and Ken Gay*
ISBN 0-7524-0119-X

**Islington**
*Gavin Smith*
ISBN 0-7524-0140-8

**Lewisham**
*John Coulter and Barry Olley*
ISBN 0-7524-0059-2

**Leyton and Leytonstone**
*Keith Romig and Peter Lawrence*
ISBN 0-7524-0158-0

**Newham Dockland**
*Howard Bloch*
ISBN 0-7524-0107-6

**Norwood**
*Nicholas Reed*
ISBN 0-7524-0147-5

**Peckham and Nunhead**
*John D. Beasley*
ISBN 0-7524-0122-X

**Piccadilly Circus**
*David Oxford*
ISBN 0-7524-0196-3

**Stoke Newington**
*Gavin Smith*
ISBN 0-7524-0159-9

**Sydenham and Forest Hill**
*John Coulter and John Seaman*
ISBN 0-7524-0036-3

**Wandsworth**
*Patrick Loobey*
ISBN 0-7524-0026-6

**Wanstead and Woodford**
*Ian Dowling and Nick Harris*
ISBN 0-7524-0113-0

## MONMOUTHSHIRE

**Vanished Abergavenny**
*Frank Olding*
ISBN 0-7524-0034-7

**Abertillery, Aberbeeg and Llanhilleth**
*Abertillery and District Museum Society and Simon Eckley*
ISBN 0-7524-0134-3

**Blaina, Nantyglo and Brynmawr**
*Trevor Rowson*
ISBN 0-7524-0136-X

## NORFOLK

**North Norfolk**
*Cliff Richard Temple*
ISBN 0-7524-0149-1

## NOTTINGHAMSHIRE

**Nottingham 1897–1947**
*Douglas Whitworth*
ISBN 0-7524-0157-2

## OXFORDSHIRE

**Banbury**
*Tom Rigby*
ISBN 0-7524-0013-4

## PEMBROKESHIRE

**Saundersfoot and Tenby**
*Ken Daniels*
ISBN 0-7524-0192-0

## RADNORSHIRE

**Llandrindod Wells**
*Chris Wilson*
ISBN 0-7524-0191-2

## SHROPSHIRE

**Leominster**
*Eric Turton*
ISBN 0-7524-0307-9

**Ludlow**
*David Lloyd*
ISBN 0-7524-0155-6

**Oswestry**
*Bernard Mitchell*
ISBN 0-7524-0032-0

**North Telford: Wellington, Oakengates, and Surrounding Areas**
*John Powell and Michael A. Vanns*
ISBN 0-7524-0124-6

**South Telford: Ironbridge Gorge, Madeley, and Dawley**
*John Powell and Michael A. Vanns*
ISBN 0-7524-0125-4

## SOMERSET

**Bath**
*Paul De'Ath*
ISBN 0-7524-0127-0

**Around Yeovil**
*Robin Ansell and Marion Barnes*
ISBN 0-7524-0178-5

## STAFFORDSHIRE

**Cannock Chase**
*Sherry Belcher and Mary Mills*
ISBN 0-7524-0051-7

**Around Cheadle**
*George Short*
ISBN 0-7524-0022-3

**The Potteries**
*Ian Lawley*
ISBN 0-7524-0046-0

**East Staffordshire**
*Geoffrey Sowerby and Richard Farman*
ISBN 0-7524-0197-1

## SUFFOLK

**Lowestoft to Southwold**
*Humphrey Phelps*
ISBN 0-7524-0108-4

**Walberswick to Felixstowe**
*Humphrey Phelps*
ISBN 0-7524-0109-2

**Around Leeds**
*Matthew Young and Dorothy Payne*
ISBN 0-7524-0168-8

**Penistone**
*Matthew Young and David Hambleton*
ISBN 0-7524-0138-6

**Selby from the William Rawling Collection**
*Matthew Young*
ISBN 0-7524-0198-X

**Central Sheffield**
*Martin Olive*
ISBN 0-7524-0011-8

**Around Stocksbridge**
*Stocksbridge and District History Society*
ISBN 0-7524-0165-3

TRANSPORT

**Filton and the Flying Machine**
*Malcolm Hall*
ISBN 0-7524-0171-8

**Gloster Aircraft Company**
*Derek James*
ISBN 0-7524-0038-X

**Great Western Swindon**
*Tim Bryan*
ISBN 0-7524-0153-X

**Midland and South Western Junction Railway**
*Mike Barnsley and Brian Bridgeman*
ISBN 0-7524-0016-9

**Shorts Aircraft**
*Mike Hooks*
ISBN 0-7524-0193-9

This stock list shows all titles available in the United Kingdom as at 30 September 1995.

# ORDER FORM

The books in this stock list are available from your local bookshop. Alternatively they are available by mail order at a totally inclusive price of £10.00 per copy.

For overseas orders please add the following postage supplement for each copy ordered:

European Union £0.36 (this includes the Republic of Ireland)
Royal Mail Zone 1 (for example, U.S.A. and Canada) £1.96
Royal Mail Zone 2 (for example, Australia and New Zealand) £2.47

Please note that all of these supplements are actual Royal Mail charges with no profit element to the Chalford Publishing Company. Furthermore, as the Air Mail Printed Papers rate applies, we are restricted from enclosing any personal correspondence other than to indicate the senders name.

Payment can be made by cheque, Visa or Mastercard. Please indicate your method of payment on this order form.

If you are not entirely happy with your purchase you may return it within 30 days of receipt for a full refund.

Please send your order to:

> The Chalford Publishing Company,
> St Mary's Mill,
> Chalford,
> Stroud,
> Gloucestershire
> GL6 8NX

This order form should perforate away from the book. However, if you are reluctant to damage the book in any way we are quite happy to accept a photocopy order form or a letter containing the necessary information.

## PLEASE WRITE CLEARLY USING BLOCK CAPITALS

Name and address of the person ordering the books listed below:

_____

_____

_____ Post code _____

Please also supply your telephone number in case we have difficulty fully understanding your requirements.     Tel.: _____ - _____

Name and address of where the books are to be despatched to (if different from above):

_____

_____

_____ Post code _____

Please indicate here if you would like to receive future information on books published by the Chalford Publishing Company.

____ Yes, please put me on your mailing list     ____ No, please just send the books ordered below

| Title | ISBN | Quantity |
|-------|------|----------|
| ................................................... | 0-7524-_____-___ | _____ |
| ................................................... | 0-7524-_____-___ | _____ |
| ................................................... | 0-7524-_____-___ | _____ |
| ................................................... | 0-7524-_____-___ | _____ |
| ................................................... | 0-7524-_____-___ | _____ |
| | Total number of books | _____ |

| | | |
|---|---|---|
| **Cost of books delivered in UK =** Number of books ordered @ £10 each | =£ | _____ |
| **Overseas postage supplement** (if relevant) | =£ | _____ |
| **TOTAL PAYMENT** | =£ | _____ |

Method of Payment          ❑ Cheque     ❑ Visa     ❑ Mastercard          **VISA**

Please make cheques payable to *The Chalford Publishing Company*          MasterCard

Name of Card Holder     _____

Card Number  ❑❑❑❑❑❑❑❑❑❑❑❑❑❑❑❑❑❑❑❑

Expiry date  ❑❑ / ❑❑

I authorise payment of £_____ from the above card

Signed _____